CHEROKEE

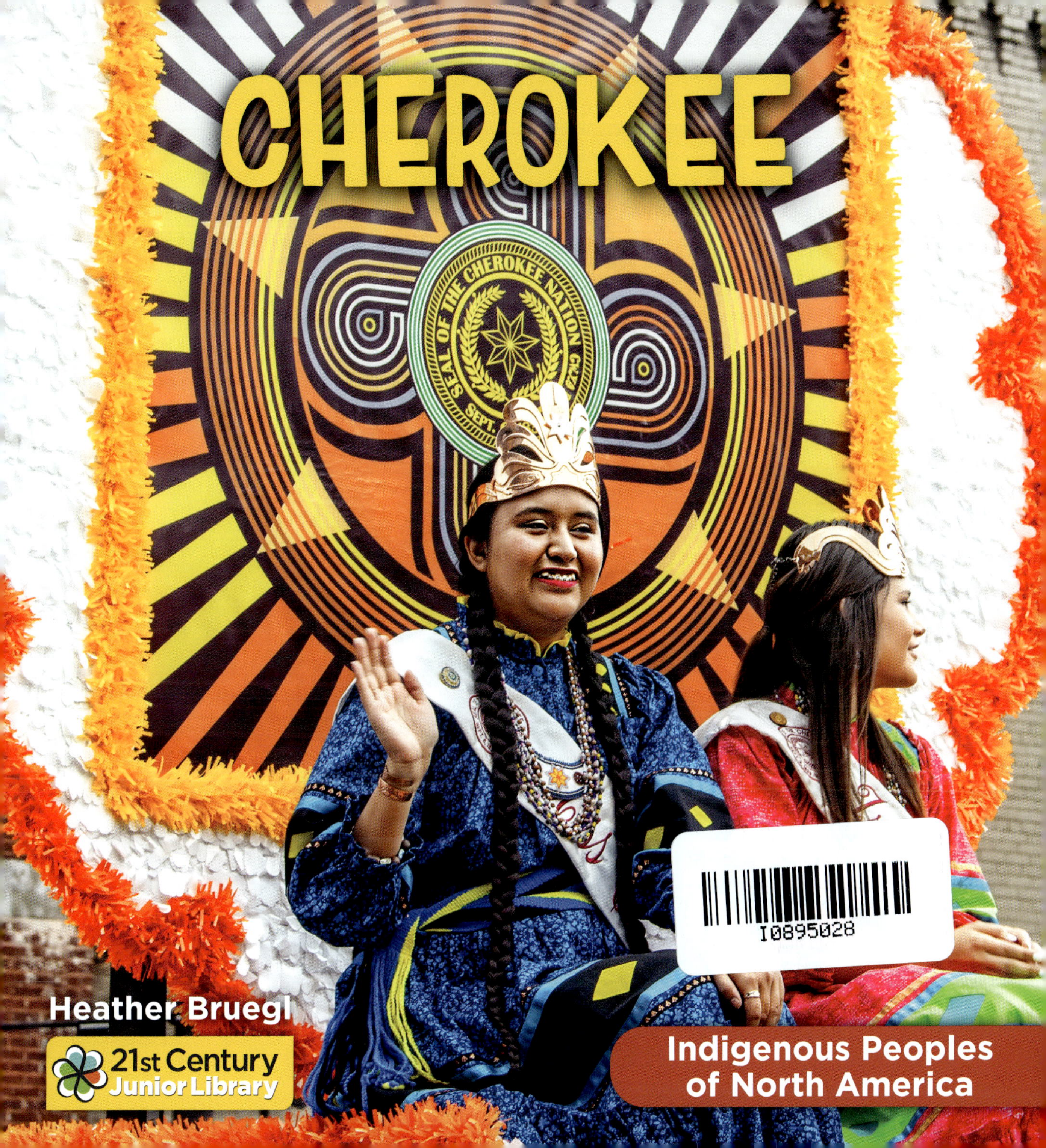

Heather Bruegl

21st Century Junior Library

Indigenous Peoples of North America

Published in the United States of America by:

Cherry Lake Press
2395 South Huron Parkway, Suite 200, Ann Arbor, Michigan 48104
www.cherrylakepress.com

Reading Adviser: Beth Walker Gambro, MS, Ed., Reading Consultant, Yorkville, IL

Photo Credits: © Aleksandr Dyskin/Dreamstime.com, cover, title page; Forest Service USDA via Flickr, 5; Architect of the Capitol, 6; © RaksyBH/Shutterstock, 9; © U.S. Army/Cover Images/Associated Press, 10; Chris Bishop/U.S. Air Force/ Department of Defense, 11; © Kim Teehee, Courtesy of Cherokee Nation Businesses, 12; © anthony heflin/Shutterstock, 15; National Park Service, 17; © Susan Vineyard/Alamy Stock Photo, 19; © Vineyard Perspective/Shutterstock, 21

Cherry Lake Press is an imprint of Cherry Lake Publishing Group.

Library of Congress Cataloging-in-Publication Data

Names: Bruegl, Heather, author.
Title: Cherokee / written by: Heather Bruegl.
Description: Ann Arbor, MI : Cherry Lake Publishing, [2025] | Series: Indigenous peoples of North America | Includes bibliographical references and index. | Audience: Grades 2-3 | Summary: "The Cherokee make up one of the largest tribal nations in the United States. In this introduction, readers will learn about Cherokee people, land, history, and accomplishments. Written by Indigenous author and public historian, Heather Bruegl, a citizen of the Oneida Nation and first-line descendent Strockbridge-Munsee, this series provides a simple and authentic introduction to the unique cultures and peoples that have made this continent home for thousands of years, and are still here today"– Provided by publisher.
Identifiers: LCCN 2024036522 | ISBN 9781668956267 (hardcover) | ISBN 9781668957110 (paperback) | 9781668957981 (ebook) | ISBN 9781668958858 (pdf)
Subjects: LCSH: Cherokee Indians–Juvenile literature.
Classification: LCC E99.C5 B88825 2025 | DDC 975.004/97557–dc23/eng/20240923
LC record available at https://lccn.loc.gov/2024036522

Cherry Lake Publishing would like to acknowledge the work of the Partnership for 21st Century Learning, a network of Battelle for Kids. Please visit Battelle for Kids online for more information.

Printed in the United States of America

About the Cover: Miss Cherokee and Miss Jr. Cherokee are titles held by Cherokee scholarship winners. The winners serve for a year as good-will ambassadors and role models for younger Cherokee girls. In the cover image, the 2019 winners ride a float in the annual National Cherokee Homecoming parade. This Cherokee Nation holiday celebrates the signing of the Cherokee Nation Constitution in 1839. It is a day of fellowship and joy.

Cherry Lake Press

CONTENTS

WHO WE ARE

The word *Cherokee* was originally a Creek word. It meant "people of a different speech." The Cherokee call themselves *Ani'-Yun'wiya'*. This means "the real people" or "the principal people." They also call themselves *Kituwa*, or *Keetoowah*. This was their first tribal name.

The Cherokee are a diverse people. They have a deep and rich history in North America. As with all peoples, there is no one way to be Cherokee. Cherokee culture continues to grow and change.

Catcuce Micco Tiger (Coche) of the Eastern Band of Cherokee Indians (EBCI) won an essay contest that saw him honored in Washington, D.C.

Make a Guess!

Why do you think cultures grow and change? Can you think of an example?

This statue of Sequoyah, an important Cherokee teacher, represents Oklahoma in the U.S. Capitol's National Statuary Hall.

From the first Indigenous written language to the first Indigenous National Aeronautics and Space Administration (**NASA**) engineer, the Cherokee have led the way to the future. Their strength and **resilience** has never changed. Today, they have one of the largest and most influential U.S. Indigenous populations.

Cherokee culture values being of a good mind. It values balance between the land and the body. This balance helps them carry on Cherokee ways.

Think!

What do you think it means to have balance? Is there something you do in your life that helps you stay balanced?

OUR LIVES TODAY

Today, there are three **federally recognized** Cherokee tribes. The largest is the Cherokee Nation in Oklahoma. Its capital is Tahlequah. The tribal enrollment is around 450,000. The United Keetoowah Band of Cherokee Indians is also headquartered in Tahlequah. The Eastern Band of Cherokee Indians have a **reservation** in Cherokee, North Carolina.

The Cherokee Nation flag

Cherokee people are teachers, artists, lawyers, police officers, craftsmen, doctors, scientists, business owners, and every job in between. Members of the Cherokee Nation live in every state. Large numbers live in Oklahoma, Texas, California, Arkansas, and Kansas. Many serve in the military and are stationed around the world.

Dwight W. Birdwell was awarded the Medal of Honor for his heroism in combat.

Look!

Look at the picture. How can you tell that Cherokee people honor military veterans?

Kim Teehee is a lawyer and political appointee who represents Cherokee interests with the U.S. government.

Cherokee people have contributed to their nation in many ways. They include Sequoyah, who created the Cherokee **syllabary**, and Wilma Mankiller, the first female principal chief of the Cherokee Nation. Physicist Jerry C. Elliott High Eagle was one of the first Indigenous NASA workers. Mary Golda Ross was the first female engineer to work for NASA. Actor and producer Wes Studi stars in major films and award-winning television series.

Create!

Research an influential Cherokee person. Make a poster display to share their accomplishments.

The ancient Appalachian Mountains and fertile valleys allowed Cherokee communities to thrive.

OUR ANCESTRAL LANDS

Cherokee ancestral lands are in the southeastern United States. They included parts of Alabama, Georgia, Tennessee, and North Carolina. Cherokee lands were lush and rich. These lands appealed to non-Indigenous settlers. When those settlers moved in, conflict often arose.

Ask Questions!

What do you want to know about Cherokee life before Europeans arrived? Ask a teacher, librarian, or other adult help you find answers to your questions.

In 1830, the U.S. Congress passed the **Indian Removal Act**. The Cherokee and other tribal nations were forced out of their homelands. The U.S. Army forced the Cherokee to move to reservations in Oklahoma. At the time, Oklahoma was called Indian Territory. Around 4,000 Cherokee men, women, and children died on the march. It became known as the Trail of Tears. In 1838, after the removal, gold was found in the Cherokee homelands.

Make a Guess!

Why might food-gathering methods have to change on a reservation? If you guessed that different food grew in the new place and different animals lived there, you'd be right!

Cherokee people today remember and honor those lost on the Trail of Tears with memorial walks.

The Cherokee found ways to care for their new lands. Like other tribal nations, they act as **stewards** of the land. Many Indigenous people believe that the land is living and breathing like the rest of us. They say people must care for it as they would for their families.

CARRYING TRADITIONS FORWARD

Before **colonization**, the Cherokee practiced many **foodways**. First and foremost, they farmed. Like many tribal nations, they planted the **Three Sisters**. These are corn, beans, and squash. They also hunted wild game. Their diets changed as colonization continued. New foods were introduced. Later, life on reservations meant that traditional food-gathering methods changed. New traditions and new traditional foods became part of Cherokee life.

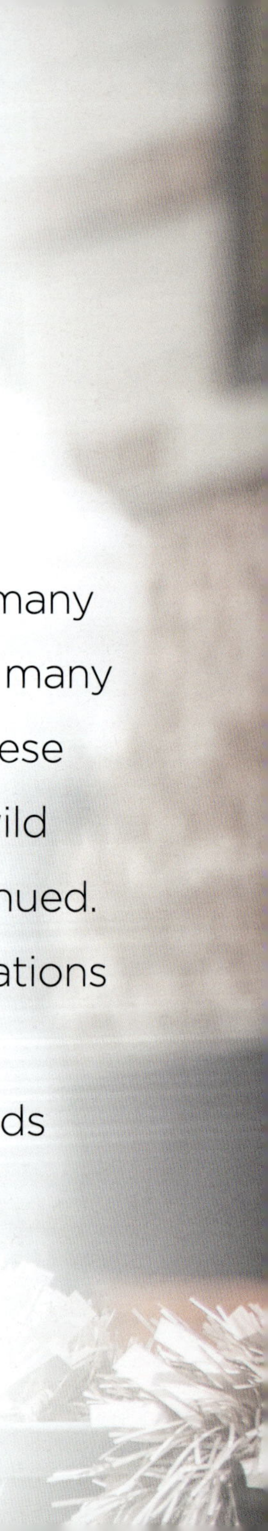

Little

At the heart of Cherokee tradition is *gadugi*, or working together. Many of the Cherokee Nation's values reflect this spirit. Health care and education programs help all community members, not just Cherokee people. Just as in the past, the Cherokee continue to work for a better future.

Cherokee military veterans and active military members serve with honor.

GLOSSARY

colonization (kah-luh-nuh-ZAY-shuhn) the act of settling in an area and exercising control over Indigenous peoples

federally recognized (FEH-druh-lee REH-kig-niezd) a status assigned to U.S. tribal nations by the federal government that provides specific rights and benefits

foodways (FOOD-wayz) the eating and cooking customs of a group of people

Indian Removal Act (IN-dee-uhn rih-MOO-vuhl AKT) a law passed in 1830 that moved tribes living in the southeastern United States to west of the Mississippi River

NASA (NAA-suh) stands for the National Aeronautics and Space Administration, the U.S. space exploration agency

reservation (reh-zuhr-VAY-shuhn) a legally designated plot of land held in trust for Indigenous peoples by the U.S. federal government

resilience (rih-ZIL-yuhns) the ability to recover from hardship or change

stewards (STOO-erds) caretakers

syllabary (SIH-luh-bair-ee) a list of symbols that stand for syllables in a language; different from an alphabet where symbols stand for individual sounds

Three Sisters (THREE SIH-sterz) a form of planting in Indigenous communities that refers to the planting of corn, beans, and squash

FIND OUT MORE

Books

Bruegl, Heather. *Indian Removal*. Ann Arbor, MI: Cherry Lake Press, 2024.

Sorell, Traci. *We Are Grateful: Otsaliheliga*. Watertown, MA: Charlesbridge, 2021.

Sorell, Traci. *We Are Still Here! Native American Truths Everyone Should Know*. Watertown, MA: Charlesbridge, 2021.

Thiele, June. *Jerry C. Elliott High Eagle*. Ann Arbor, MI: Cherry Lake Press, 2022.

Online

With an adult, explore more online with these suggested searches.

- "Native Voices | Cherokee Nation," PBS Learning Media
- "Culture & History: A Thriving Nation," Visit Cherokee Nation

Say Hello!

Osiyo (oh-see-oh) is "hello" in Cherokee. It carries a deep spiritual meaning of welcome and hospitality.

INDEX

ABOUT THE AUTHOR

Heather Bruegl, a member of the Oneida Nation of Wisconsin/Stockbridge-Munsee, is a Madonna University graduate with a Master of Arts in U.S. History. She is a public historian and decolonial educator, and her Munsee name is Kiishookunkwe, which means “Sunflower in Full Bloom.” Heather frequently travels to present on Indigenous history, policy, and activism, bringing her deep knowledge and personal connection to the subject.